ESFJ: THE CARING CONNECTOR

The ESFJ Guide to Meaningful Living

Asa Eccleston Kibilski

CONTENTS

THE ESFJ BLUEPRINT: DECODING YOUR CORE TRAITS

If you identify as an ESFJ (Extraverted, Sensing, Feeling, Judging), you belong to a personality type known for its warmth, conscientiousness, and extraordinary social skills. ESFJs, often nicknamed "Providers" or "Consuls," are the heart and soul of many communities, families, and workplaces. Their natural inclination towards service, paired with their innate ability to understand and connect with others, makes them invaluable members of society.

At the core of the ESFJ personality lies a potent combination of cognitive functions. Let's break down these key components that shape your perspective and drive your behavior:

- **Extraverted Feeling (Fe):** Your dominant function is Extraverted Feeling, making empathy and social harmony your superpowers. You are deeply attuned to the emotions and needs of others. You find joy in creating a sense of belonging and fostering positive connections. Decisions are often guided by a desire to maintain the wellbeing of those around you.

- **Introverted Sensing (Si):** Your auxiliary function, Introverted Sensing, grounds you in the present and provides a strong connection to past experiences. You value tradition, routine, and rely on what you know has worked well before. Details and practicalities are important to you, leading to a strong sense of organization and reliability.

- **Extraverted Intuition (Ne):** This tertiary function allows you to see possibilities and envision different scenarios. While not your primary mode of operation, Ne helps you brainstorm, find creative solutions, and consider various perspectives when making decisions or helping others.

- **Introverted Thinking (Ti):** As your inferior function, Introverted Thinking represents a less developed area. You may find yourself less drawn to logical analysis or theoretical frameworks. However, as you mature, Ti can help you create internal systems, prioritize efficiency, and balance emotion with reason.

The ESFJ in Action

The combination of these functions manifests in several defining strengths characteristic of ESFJs. You likely possess a deep desire for social connection and a knack for reading people. Practical problem-solving comes naturally, as does a drive to organize your environment and the lives of those around you. A strong work ethic and dedication to fulfilling your responsibilities are common hallmarks of this personality type.

However, like any personality type, ESFJs also face a unique set of challenges. Overextending yourself to please others, an aversion to conflict, and a sensitivity to criticism can create hurdles. Understanding these tendencies allows you to work with them instead of against them.

This first chapter sets the stage for the rest of the book. As we delve deeper, we'll unpack the nuances of the ESFJ personality, explore common strengths and weaknesses, and provide practical tools for personal growth and maximizing your extraordinary potential as a Caring Connector.

THE WARMTH FACTOR: UNDERSTANDING YOUR EMPATHY SUPERPOWER

If there's a single word that encapsulates the essence of an ESFJ, it's 'empathy'. Your dominant function, Extraverted Feeling (Fe), acts as an emotional radar, constantly scanning your environment and absorbing the feelings of those around you. This superpower allows you to intuit others' needs, celebrate their joys, and share their sorrows with an authenticity that draws people to you.

How ESFJ Empathy Manifests

Your empathy shows up in countless ways, both big and small:

- **The Comforting Presence:** You instinctively know how to offer a listening ear, a warm hug, or a thoughtful word that soothes someone going through a difficult time. People feel seen and understood in your presence.
- **The Social Glue:** You thrive in group settings, effortlessly facilitating introductions, making everyone feel included, and diffusing tension with your easygoing nature.
- **The Master of Practical Support:** You don't just empathize —you act on it. Whether it's organizing a meal train for a sick neighbor, helping a friend with a project, or throwing a surprise party, you find immense joy in offering tangible help.
- **The Guardian of Harmony:** You're acutely aware of social dynamics and disharmony sends shivers down your spine. You'll often go out of your way to mediate conflicts, smooth ruffled feathers, and restore a sense of peace.

The Benefits of High Fe

Your extraordinary empathy brings countless benefits to your life and the lives of others:

- **Strong Relationships:** Your ability to connect on a deep level fosters strong, lasting bonds in friendships, romantic relationships, and family life.
- **Natural Caregivers:** You excel in roles that require compassion and a service-oriented mindset, such as nursing, teaching, counseling, or social work.
- **Community Builders:** You have the potential to be a powerful force for good, bringing people together, championing social causes, and creating a sense of belonging wherever you go.

The Potential Pitfalls of Empathy

While a powerful gift, unchecked empathy can also lead to challenges for ESFJs:

- **Emotional Burnout:** Absorbing the emotions of others can be draining. If you don't learn to set boundaries, you risk empathy fatigue and burnout.
- **People-Pleasing:** The desire to make everyone happy can lead to overextending yourself, saying 'yes' when you should say 'no,' and neglecting your own needs.
- **Sensitivity to Criticism:** Because you deeply care about others' opinions, harsh words or negative feedback can cut deep, potentially leading to self-doubt.
- **Internalizing Others' Problems:** It's easy to blur the lines between your own emotions and those of the people around you, leading to unnecessary stress and anxiety.

Cultivating Healthy Empathy

The key is not to diminish your empathy, but to learn how to manage it effectively:

- **Self-Awareness:** Pay attention to your energy levels and emotional state. Learn to recognize the signs when you're becoming overwhelmed.

- **Boundaries:** It's okay to say 'no' and prioritize your own needs. This doesn't make you selfish; it allows you to be there for others from a place of strength, not depletion.
- **Self-Care:** Schedule time for activities that recharge you, whether it's a quiet walk in nature, a relaxing hobby, or simply some time alone to decompress.
- **Mindfulness:** Practicing mindfulness can help you stay present and avoid getting swept away by the emotional currents of others.

Remember, your empathy is a precious gift. By learning to harness it with self-awareness and healthy boundaries, you become a powerful force for good, both in your own life and in the world around you.

HARMONY SEEKERS: ESFJS AND THE DESIRE FOR CONNECTION

ESFJs crave connection like a plant craves sunlight. You are intrinsically wired to build bridges, foster belonging, and create harmonious environments where people feel valued and understood. This deep-seated drive stems from your dominant Extraverted Feeling (Fe) function, which prioritizes the emotional well-being of your social circle.

How the Need for Harmony Manifests

Your desire for connection shows up in various facets of your life:

- **The Social Butterfly:** You thrive in bustling environments, effortlessly striking up conversations, remembering details about people's lives, and making others feel at ease. Parties, gatherings, and community events are where you come alive.
- **The Bridge Builder:** You spot disconnects and have a knack for bringing people together. Whether it's introducing new friends, organizing social events, or playing peacemaker during a disagreement, you facilitate a sense of unity and belonging.
- **The Cheerleader:** You're the ultimate supporter, celebrating the milestones of those around you with genuine enthusiasm. You have a way of making people feel seen, appreciated, and encouraged to shine.
- **Tradition Keeper:** You cherish rituals, family gatherings, and holiday celebrations that reinforce bonds and create lasting memories. Preserving these traditions helps you feel connected to your roots and provides a sense of continuity.

The Benefits of Craving Connection

Your inherent need for harmony brings many positives to your life and the lives of others:

- **Deep, Enduring Relationships:** You invest time and effort into your friendships, romantic partnerships, and family bonds, resulting in strong, enriching relationships that stand the test of time.
- **Community Pillars:** You're often the go-to person for organizing events, volunteering in your community, or lending a helping hand. Your efforts create a sense of togetherness and belonging.
- **Natural Networkers:** Your ability to connect with diverse people opens doors for yourself and others, both personally and professionally.
- **Empathetic Leaders:** In leadership roles, you excel at fostering team spirit, recognizing individual contributions, and motivating others through genuine appreciation.

Potential Challenges of Seeking Harmony

- **Conflict Avoidance:** Your distaste for disharmony can sometimes lead to sidestepping necessary but difficult conversations. While well-intentioned, this can create unresolved issues that fester over time.
- **Overextending Yourself:** In your eagerness to foster connection, you might overcommit, spreading yourself too thin, and risking neglecting your own needs for rest and personal time.
- **Fear of Disapproval:** Your desire to be liked and maintain a positive atmosphere could lead you to downplay your own opinions or needs to avoid rocking the boat.
- **Loneliness Vulnerability:** When connections falter, or you find yourself isolated, ESFJs can feel a profound sense of loneliness and disconnection due to their reliance on social interaction for emotional well-being.

Striking a Balance

The key lies in finding a healthy balance between your desire for harmony and your own needs for authenticity and self-preservation. Here are a few tips:

- **Learn to Address Conflict Constructively:** Recognize that respectful disagreement can be healthy and lead to growth. Develop skills in assertive communication and conflict resolution.
- **Embrace "Alone Time":** Schedule moments of solitude for reflection and recharging. Don't equate being alone with loneliness.
- **Cultivate Diverse Interests:** Develop hobbies and passions outside of your social circle. This fosters a sense of individuality and gives you something to fall back on during times of social isolation.
- **Be Authentic:** While empathy is your superpower, don't feel pressured to be someone you're not in order to please others. True connection comes from sharing your genuine self.

Remember, a strong desire for connection is a beautiful trait. By embracing this aspect of your nature, while simultaneously nurturing your individuality and healthy boundaries, you can create both fulfilling social bonds and a deep sense of peace within yourself.

PRACTICAL IDEALISTS: BALANCING HEART AND STRUCTURE

ESFJs are a fascinating paradox. You possess a deeply empathetic heart driven by a desire for harmony and connection, yet you also have a practical, grounded side that craves order and stability. This unique blend of heart and structure is what makes you both a compassionate visionary and a reliable doer.

The Practical Side of the ESFJ

Your auxiliary function, Introverted Sensing (Si), provides a strong counterbalance to your dominant Extraverted Feeling. Here's how it manifests:

- **Detail-Oriented:** You pay attention to the specifics, ensuring tasks are completed accurately and nothing slips through the cracks.
- **Reliability personified:** If you say you'll do something, consider it done. You pride yourself on following through on commitments and meeting deadlines.
- **Drawn to Routine:** Predictable schedules and familiar processes offer a sense of comfort and security. You find efficiency and satisfaction in tried-and-true methods.
- **Appreciation for Tradition:** You hold a respect for tradition, finding value in customs, rituals, and the wisdom passed down through generations.

The Idealistic Side of the ESFJ

While your practical side keeps you grounded, your Extraverted Feeling fuels a streak of idealism:

- **A Better World Visionary:** You're not satisfied with simply maintaining the status quo. You envision a world where everyone feels cared for, supported, and valued.

- **Guided by Core Values:** Strong moral convictions shape your actions and decisions. Fairness, kindness, and helping those in need are guiding principles.
- **Socially Conscious:** You're likely drawn to causes that fight for social justice, equality, or community well-being.
- **Belief in People:** You have a fundamental belief in the potential of others, inspiring them to be the best versions of themselves.

When Heart and Structure Collide

The potential for internal tension arises when your deep-seated ideals clash with the realities of the world. You might find yourself frustrated when things don't go according to plan, systems feel inefficient, or people act selfishly. Striking the right balance is key.

Tips for Embracing Your Practical Idealism

- **Focus on Sustainable Progress:** Recognize that change doesn't happen overnight. Set realistic goals and celebrate small wins along the way.
- **Channel Idealism into Action:** Instead of dwelling on imperfections, put your energy into practical solutions that make a tangible difference in your community or workplace.
- **Find Like-Minded People:** Surround yourself with people who share your values and commitment to positive change. Collaborating with others amplifies your impact.
- **Avoid Perfectionism:** Striving for excellence is admirable, but perfection is unattainable. Learn to embrace "good enough" and avoid getting bogged down in excessive details.

The Beauty of Your Duality

Your blend of practicality and idealism is a potent force for good. You have the heart to envision a better world and the hands to help build it. Here's how this unique combination benefits you:

- **Grounded Empathy:** Your practical side prevents your empathy from becoming unfocused or overwhelming. You know how to turn compassion into action.
- **Realistic Optimism:** You're able to maintain hope while acknowledging real-world constraints. This helps you stay motivated and avoid becoming disillusioned.
- **Transformational Leadership:** You inspire others by showing them how to translate values into concrete actions that improve situations or the lives of others.

By understanding and appreciating both sides of your nature, you maximize your potential for personal growth and meaningful contribution to the world around you.

THE PEOPLE-PLEASING PARADOX: SETTING HEALTHY BOUNDARIES

One of the most common struggles faced by ESFJs is the tendency to put the needs of others above their own. Driven by your deep-seated empathy and desire for harmony, you may find yourself saying "yes" too often, overextending yourself, and neglecting your own well-being. This is what we call the People-Pleasing Paradox.

Why ESFJs People-Please

There are several reasons why ESFJs fall into this pattern:

- **The Core Need for Approval:** Your Extraverted Feeling (Fe) makes you acutely attuned to how others perceive you. You crave validation and fear disapproval, making it hard to say "no" even when you're overwhelmed.
- **Harmony at Any Cost:** Your aversion to conflict can lead you to sacrifice your own needs to keep the peace. You may avoid expressing differing opinions or voicing disagreements for fear of upsetting someone.
- **Misplaced Responsibility:** You often feel a strong sense of responsibility for the well-being of those around you. This can make you take on burdens that aren't yours to carry.
- **Confusing Selflessness with Self-Worth:** Your natural inclination towards service might lead to a belief that your value stems from what you do for others, not from who you inherently are.

The Consequences of Overextending Yourself

While well-intentioned, chronic people-pleasing has several negative consequences:

- **Burnout:** Constantly pouring from an empty cup leads to emotional exhaustion, physical fatigue, and a loss of joy.
- **Resentment:** Over time, as you neglect your own needs, resentment can creep in, damaging relationships with others and yourself.
- **Decreased Self-Esteem:** If your self-worth is solely tied to external validation, you'll always feel dependent on the approval of others, leaving you vulnerable to self-doubt.
- **Missed Opportunities:** When you're always focused on pleasing others, you may miss out on pursuing your own passions, goals, and personal growth.

The Power of Healthy Boundaries

Setting healthy boundaries is the antidote to people-pleasing. Boundaries define where you end and others begin. They help you protect your time, energy, and emotional well-being, without compromising your compassionate nature.

How to Start Setting Boundaries

- **Self-Awareness is Key:** Pay attention to the physical and emotional signals that tell you you're overextended. Learn to recognize the patterns that lead to people-pleasing.
- **Permission to Say "No":** You are allowed to decline requests without feeling guilty or having to give lengthy explanations. A simple "No, I can't do that right now" is sufficient.
- **Start Small:** Begin with low-stakes situations to practice boundary setting. Gradually build your confidence as you experience positive outcomes.
- **Communicate Kindly but Firmly:** Express your needs assertively but with compassion. For example, "I'd love to help, but my schedule is full this week. Could we explore alternative options?"
- **Don't Expect Overnight Change:** This is a process of rewiring deeply ingrained habits. Be patient with yourself,

and celebrate even small steps forward.

Remember: Boundaries are an Act of Self-Love

Setting boundaries might feel uncomfortable at first, especially if you're used to accommodating others at your own expense. However, remember these points:

- **Boundaries Enhance Relationships:** Healthy boundaries actually lead to stronger, more authentic relationships based on mutual respect.
- **You Can Still Be Caring:** Setting boundaries doesn't make you selfish. It allows you to be there for others from a place of strength and sustainability.
- **Self-Respect Attracts Respect:** When you prioritize your own needs, you teach others how to treat you, ultimately earning their genuine respect.

By breaking free from the people-pleasing paradox, you free yourself to live a more fulfilling and balanced life. You'll have the energy and clarity to nurture meaningful connections, pursue your own goals, and offer your gifts to the world with genuine joy, not from a place of depletion.

SENSITIVE SOULS: NAVIGATING CRITICISM AND SEEKING VALIDATION

ESFJs, with your big hearts and desire to connect with others, you are often deeply sensitive individuals. While your empathy and social intelligence are incredible strengths, this sensitivity can also make you vulnerable to criticism and reliant on external validation. Understanding this aspect of yourself is key to maintaining emotional balance and fostering self-confidence.

Why ESFJs Are Sensitive to Criticism

Several factors contribute to your sensitivity:

- **Fe Dominance:** Your dominant Extraverted Feeling (Fe) makes you highly attuned to the emotions and opinions of others. Negative feedback can cut deep because you genuinely care about how others perceive you.
- **Harmony Seekers:** As natural harmony seekers, criticism disrupts the sense of social balance you value deeply. It can feel like a personal attack, even if it's constructive.
- **Internalized Ideals:** You hold yourself to high standards and strive for excellence. When you fall short of your own expectations (or perceive that others see you as falling short) it can trigger feelings of inadequacy.
- **Fear of Disapproval:** Your desire to be liked and accepted can make negative feedback feel threatening, leaving you worried about damaging relationships.

The Need for External Validation

Closely tied to your sensitivity to criticism is a need for external validation. Here's why:

- **Validating Your Worth:** When so much of your identity is tied to helping and pleasing others, your self-esteem can hinge on positive feedback and recognition from the outside.
- **Fe's Need for Resonance:** Extraverted Feeling thrives on feeling understood and appreciated. A lack of positive reinforcement can lead you to question your actions and worth.
- **Confusing Service with Value:** Because you're wired to serve, it's easy to forget that your value is inherent, not solely dependent on what you do for others.

Navigating Criticism Constructively

Here's how to handle both well-deserved and unfair criticism with grace:

- **Separate Facts from Feelings:** Try to distinguish between objective feedback and emotional reactions. Focus on the practical information that might help you improve.
- **Consider the Source:** Is the criticism coming from someone you trust and respect? Is it delivered with constructive intent, or is it intentionally hurtful? This context matters.
- **Don't Take it Personally:** Remember, criticism often reflects more about the person giving it than about you. Avoid internalizing negativity.
- **Self-Compassion:** Practice kindness towards yourself, especially when you feel hurt. Remind yourself of your strengths and the positive impact you have on others.

Cultivating Inner Validation

To break free from the validation trap, focus on self-reliance:

- **Celebrate Your Wins:** Keep a list of your accomplishments, big and small. Refer back to it when you feel self-doubt creeping in.
- **Reframe Your Focus:** Shift from seeking external approval to seeking alignment with your own values. Did you act with

integrity and kindness? That's what truly matters.

- **Nurture Self-Trust:** Build confidence in your own judgment by making decisions independently and reflecting on the outcomes.
- **Define Your Own Success:** What does a meaningful life look like to you, regardless of anyone else's opinions? Anchor yourself in these personal goals.

Remember: Your Sensitivity is a Strength

Your sensitive nature, when paired with self-awareness, can be a tremendous asset:

- **Deeply Empathetic:** Your sensitivity allows you to understand and connect with others on a profound level.
- **Conscientious and Considerate:** You care deeply about doing the right thing and treating others with respect.
- **Motivated to Grow:** The desire to improve fuels personal development and learning, allowing you to refine your skills and character.

By learning to manage your sensitivity to criticism and cultivate a strong sense of internal validation, you'll unlock greater emotional resilience and self-confidence. Embrace your sensitive soul as a core part of who you are, and use it to navigate your journey with both strength and compassion.

ESFJS IN LOVE: BUILDING NURTURING RELATIONSHIPS

ESFJs, with your warmth, loyalty, and natural caregiving instincts, are wired for connection and thrive in committed relationships. You long for deep emotional bonds, security, and a sense of belonging. Let's delve into how your personality type shapes your approach to love and partnerships.

What ESFJs Seek in a Partner

As an ESFJ, you are likely drawn to partners who offer:

- **Emotional Connection:** You crave genuine affection, open communication, and the ability to share your feelings and experiences without fear of judgment.
- **Shared Values:** A partner who aligns with your core values, such as honesty, kindness, and commitment, builds a strong foundation for trust and respect.
- **Appreciation:** Feeling valued and having your contributions recognized is essential. Words of affirmation are incredibly meaningful to you.
- **Stability and Commitment:** You seek a partner who is also looking for a long-term, stable partnership. Predictability and loyalty provide a sense of security.

The Strengths ESFJs Bring to Relationships

You offer an abundance of positive qualities that make you a loving and supportive partner:

- **Nurturers at Heart:** You take joy in caring for loved ones and creating a warm, welcoming home environment. Acts of service are a natural expression of your love.
- **Loyal and Devoted:** When you commit to someone, you're in it for the long haul. You value faithfulness and work hard to

keep your promises.

- **Excellent Communicators (Usually):** You generally express your feelings and needs openly, and you're a good listener. This helps create a strong foundation for healthy communication.
- **Conflict Minimizers:** While you dislike disharmony, you're usually willing to compromise and work towards solutions to keep the relationship peaceful.

Potential Challenges in Love

Like any personality type, ESFJs face certain challenges in relationships:

- **People-Pleasing Tendencies:** Your desire to please might lead to suppressing your own needs or avoiding disagreements for the sake of keeping the peace.
- **Sensitivity to Criticism:** Even well-intended feedback from your partner can sting deeply, requiring open communication and reassurance.
- **Jealousy Struggles:** Your need for validation could lead to feelings of jealousy or insecurity if you perceive your partner's attention is elsewhere.
- **Expecting Perfection:** Holding yourself and your partner to unrealistic standards can create tension and disappointment.

Tips for Building Healthy Partnerships

Here's how to foster strong, fulfilling bonds:

- **Maintain Your Individuality:** Don't lose yourself in the relationship. Cultivate your own interests, friendships, and personal growth to avoid codependency.
- **Communicate Honest Needs:** Don't expect your partner to be a mind-reader. Express your needs clearly and without fear of causing disappointment.
- **Address Conflict Head-On:** Develop healthy conflict resolution tactics. Learn to voice disagreements respectfully

and work towards solutions collaboratively.

- **Realistic Expectations:** Embrace the fact that no one is perfect, including you. Focus on appreciating your partner's positive qualities.
- **Self-Love is Key:** A strong sense of self-worth and internal validation guards against insecurities and allows you to fully enjoy the love you deserve.

Compatibility Considerations

While ESFJs can find happiness with various personality types, there's often strong compatibility with partners who:

- **Share Your Values:** Types like ISFJ, ISTJ, or ESFP often share similar ideals on commitment, family, and tradition.
- **Balance Your Practicality:** Intuitive types (NFs or NTs) can add a spark of spontaneity and new perspectives, expanding your worldview.
- **Offer Emotional Security:** Feeling types (xSFx) can match your depth of emotion and desire for connection.

The Beauty of ESFJ Love

ESFJs have the potential to build incredibly nurturing and supportive relationships. Your warmth, loyalty, and commitment to fostering connection make you a cherished partner. By being mindful of your potential pitfalls and actively nurturing a healthy, balanced relationship dynamic, you can find profound love and create a lasting, fulfilling bond.

FRIENDSHIP POWERHOUSE: THE ART OF CONNECTING WITH OTHERS

If friendship were a competitive sport, ESFJs would be gold medalists. You possess a natural talent for building strong, enduring connections and fostering a sense of belonging. Your empathy, warmth, and genuine interest in others make you the friend everyone wants by their side.

The ESFJ Friendship Style

Your approach to friendship is characterized by:

- **Initiative and Inclusivity:** You're the one reaching out, planning gatherings, and making sure everyone feels welcome. You're a master at making introductions and bridging social gaps.
- **The Ultimate Cheerleader:** You're quick to celebrate milestones, offer heartfelt encouragement, and remind your friends of their strengths when they're feeling down.
- **Deeply Loyal:** You stick by your friends through thick and thin, prioritizing your relationships and making time for those you care about.
- **Practical Support:** Whether it's a listening ear, a helping hand, or a home-cooked meal in times of need, you're the friend who goes the extra mile.
- **The Memory Keeper:** You cherish shared experiences, remembering birthdays, anniversaries, and inside jokes that reinforce the special bond of friendship.

Why People Are Drawn to ESFJ Friends

Your unique blend of qualities makes you incredibly attractive as a friend:

- **The Emotional Safe Space:** People feel emotionally seen, heard, and understood in your presence. They know they can confide in you without judgment.
- **The Fun Instigator:** While deeply caring, you also know how to have a good time, injecting a dose of lightness and spontaneity into social gatherings.
- **The Shoulder to Cry On:** You possess an empathetic heart and intuitive sense of what your friends need during difficult times, offering unwavering support.
- **Community Catalyst:** You're the glue that holds friend groups together, effortlessly organizing events and outings that create cherished memories.

Potential Friendship Challenges

Like any personality type, ESFJs can encounter some bumps in the friendship road:

- **Overextending Yourself:** Your desire to be there for everyone can lead to burnout and neglecting your own needs for rest and personal space.
- **Unrealistic Expectations:** Sometimes you might hold friends to unrealistically high standards, feeling let down when they don't meet your expectations of perfect support.
- **Possessiveness:** Your loyalty, while admirable, could sometimes feel stifling for more independent friends.
- **Sensitivity to Rejection:** Any perceived coldness or distance from a friend could wound deeply, even if unintended.

Tips for Fostering Healthy Friendships

- **Set Boundaries:** It's okay to say "no" sometimes. True friends understand and respect your need to recharge and put your own well-being first.
- **Accept Imperfections:** Embrace your friends for who they are, flaws and all. Avoid the trap of perfectionism, which can hinder connection.
- **Balance Giving and Receiving:** Nurturing friendships

should be reciprocal. Make sure you're also receiving support and encouragement from your circle of friends.

- **Open Communication:** If feeling hurt or misunderstood, initiate an honest conversation with your friend from a place of compassion and understanding.

The Power of Diverse Friendships

While ESFJs are social butterflies, it's essential to cultivate friendships with various personality types. Friends who possess different strengths expand your horizons and offer valuable perspectives:

- **Intuitive Types (NFs or NTs):** Deep thinkers can stimulate intellectual conversations and inspire you to see the world from fresh angles.
- **Introverted Friends:** Friends requiring less social interaction offer balance and a chance to recharge your energy without the pressure to always entertain.
- **More Independent Types:** Friends with a strong sense of individuality can encourage you to nurture your own hobbies and passions.

The Gift of ESFJ Friendship

ESFJs are friendship powerhouses, enriching the lives of those around them. Your warmth, loyalty, and ability to foster a sense of belonging are true gifts. Embrace your talents as a connector, consciously address any potential challenges, and cherish the diverse, fulfilling friendships that blossom in your life.

FAMILY TIES: ESFJS AS PARENTS, SIBLINGS, AND CHILDREN

ESFJs place immense value on family bonds. Whether you're a parent, a sibling, a child, or a member of an extended family, you approach these roles with your trademark warmth, dedication, and desire to create a loving and harmonious environment for everyone.

ESFJs as Parents

You are natural nurturers, making parenthood a profound and fulfilling role. Here's how your ESFJ qualities shine as a parent:

- **The Heart of the Home:** You create a warm, loving atmosphere where your children feel safe, supported, and deeply cherished.
- **Tradition Keepers:** Family rituals, holidays, and shared experiences are important to you, building a strong sense of history and belonging for your children.
- **Practical Providers:** You take great care to meet your children's physical needs, ensuring they are well-fed, clothed, and have a comfortable, secure home.
- **Moral Guides:** Instilling strong values and a sense of right and wrong is essential to you. You lead by example, teaching your children kindness, empathy, and responsibility.
- **Devoted Cheerleaders:** You're your children's biggest fans, encouraging their dreams and celebrating their accomplishments with genuine enthusiasm.

Potential Parenting Challenges

- **Overprotection:** The desire to shield your children from hardship could inadvertently stifle their independence and ability to learn from mistakes.

- **Perfectionism Pitfalls:** Holding yourself and your children to unrealistic standards can create undue pressure and anxiety.
- **Sensitivity to Criticism:** Parenting advice, even well-intentioned, can feel like a personal attack. Discernment between constructive and unhelpful feedback is key.
- **Struggles with Autonomy:** As your children grow, adjusting to their increasing need for independence and individual decision-making can be challenging.

Parenting Tips

- **Encourage Exploration:** Strike a balance between nurturing and allowing for safe, age-appropriate risk-taking to foster independence and confidence.
- **Practice Flexibility:** Accept that there are multiple "right" ways to do things. Relaxing rigid expectations helps create a more peaceful home.
- **Open Communication:** Create a safe space for your children to express their feelings, both positive and negative, without judgment.
- **Model Self-Care:** Show your children the importance of prioritizing their own well-being, not just the needs of others.

ESFJs as Siblings

You're likely to be a supportive, and encouraging sibling. You often exhibit these traits:

- **Protective Instincts:** You look out for your siblings, especially younger ones, and are fiercely loyal to them.
- **Peacekeepers:** You try to keep things harmonious between siblings, playing mediator when conflicts arise.
- **Memory Makers:** You cherish shared experiences, creating traditions, and remembering funny inside jokes with your siblings.
- **Connectors:** You facilitate strong bonds amongst all siblings,

ensuring everyone feels included and cared for.

ESFJs as Children

As a child, you're likely to be well-liked, responsible, and eager to please:

- **Adults' Helper:** You love feeling useful and offering assistance to parents, teachers, and other adults in your life.
- **Rule Follower:** You respect authority figures and thrive in environments with clear structure and expectations.
- **Approval Seeker:** Positive reinforcement and validation boost your confidence and inspire you to do your best.
- **Social Butterfly:** You enjoy being around other kids and make friends easily.

Family Dynamics & the ESFJ

ESFJs thrive in warm, close-knit families. Your dedication to tradition, loyalty, and practical support makes you a cornerstone. However, remember:

- **Healthy Boundaries Matter:** Even with family, it's okay to say "no" and prioritize your own needs for self-care and personal space.
- **Embrace Differences:** Not everyone in your family will share your values or approach things the same way. Cultivate acceptance and respect for diversity.
- **Perfection Isn't the Goal:** A loving, supportive family doesn't have to be perfect to be wonderful. Focus on the positive bonds you share.

ESFJs bring a unique blend of warmth, practicality, and tradition to their family roles. With a dash of self-awareness and a willingness to adapt as your family evolves, you can foster strong, supportive, and deeply fulfilling bonds that last a lifetime.

THE CAREER COMPASS: FINDING FULFILLING ROLES

ESFJs, with your people-oriented nature, practical skills, and strong work ethic, have the potential to thrive in a variety of careers. Your success lies in finding roles that align with your core values, capitalize on your strengths, and offer opportunities for genuine connection and contribution.

Fields that Suit ESFJs

ESFJs often excel in careers that emphasize:

- **Helping Others:** Fields like healthcare, social work, counseling, non-profit work, and human resources allow you to use your empathy and service orientation to make a direct impact on people's lives.
- **Education & Childcare:** Your nurturing, organized nature shines in roles like teaching (especially elementary levels), early childhood education, or special needs support, where you guide and positively influence young minds.
- **Community-Centered Work:** Careers like event planning, public relations, customer service, or administrative roles in community organizations let you facilitate connections and ensure smooth operations for the benefit of others.
- **Structured & Detail-Oriented Roles:** Positions in fields like office management, accounting, logistics, or project coordination suit your preference for organization, predictability, and following established processes.
- **Creative Expression:** While less obvious, ESFJs with artistic or expressive inclinations can find fulfillment in design, photography, music, or culinary-related fields where your work enhances others' lives.

ESFJ Work Environment Preferences

Beyond specific roles, consider what work environments best suit your personality:

- **Collaborative:** You thrive in team-oriented settings where there's a sense of camaraderie and cooperation towards shared goals.
- **People-Focused:** Jobs involving regular interaction with colleagues, clients, or the public keep you energized and fulfilled.
- **Values-Driven:** Working for an organization whose mission aligns with your own values provides a deeper sense of purpose.
- **Structure with Flexibility:** You appreciate a framework of guidelines but need some autonomy to manage your workload and exercise your problem-solving skills.
- **Appreciation & Recognition:** Feeling valued and having your contributions acknowledged is crucial for your morale and job satisfaction.

Potential Workplace Challenges

- **Repetitive Tasks:** Overly mundane, repetitive work can become draining for ESFJs who crave human interaction and variety.
- **Highly Competitive Environments:** Cutthroat competition or a lack of team spirit can clash with your desire for harmony and collaboration.
- **Undervalued or Invisible Work:** Roles where your contributions go unnoticed or feel unappreciated can lead to long-term frustration.
- **Conflict Overload:** While you prefer harmony, jobs requiring frequent conflict management or handling difficult personalities might be emotionally taxing.
- **Inflexible Systems:** Rigid workplaces with little room for creative input or process improvement could stifle your need to offer solutions.

Career Success Strategies

- **Focus on Your Strengths:** Capitalize on your natural warmth, communication skills, organization, and follow-through in your job search and within your role.
- **Seek Growth Opportunities:** Look for jobs offering professional development, allowing you to learn new skills and avoid stagnation.
- **Advocate for Yourself:** Don't be afraid to ask for recognition when deserved, negotiate salary and benefits, or request adjustments to your workload if feeling overwhelmed.
- **Network & Build Relationships:** Your knack for connecting with others is an asset! Proactively build professional relationships, as opportunities often arise through your network.
- **Find a Mentor:** A mentor with experience in your field can offer valuable insights, support, and guidance for career advancement.

Remember: Fulfillment is Personal

There's no single "perfect" career path for all ESFJs. Consider these points:

- **Values Alignment:** What truly matters to you? Is it helping people, community impact, security, or leaving a creative mark? Let your values guide you.
- **Passion Points:** What activities are you drawn to outside of work? Exploring hobbies can sometimes lead to unexpected career paths.
- **Lifestyle Balance:** Consider your desired work-life balance. Some ESFJs will thrive in demanding careers, while others prioritize flexibility for family and personal time.

Finding a career that lights you up is an ongoing journey of self-discovery. By embracing your strengths, seeking work that aligns with your values, and actively managing potential challenges, you can create a professional life that brings both satisfaction and a deep sense of purpose.

TEAM PLAYERS EXTRAORDINAIRE: THRIVING IN COLLABORATIVE WORKPLACES

ESFJs are natural team players. Your genuine desire to contribute, support others, and work towards a common goal makes you a highly valued asset in collaborative environments. Let's delve into the specific strengths you bring to a team dynamic.

How ESFJs Excel in Team Settings

- **Social Lubricant:** You ease tensions, facilitate introductions, and foster a sense of camaraderie with your warmth and open communication.
- **Practical Problem-Solver:** You're adept at identifying logistical issues, creating realistic action plans, and ensuring tasks are completed efficiently and on time.
- **Harmonizers:** Your conflict-averse nature drives you to find compromises and solutions that keep everyone on board and the team morale high.
- **Morale Boosters:** You naturally recognize and celebrate team members' contributions, making everyone feel valued and appreciated.
- **Detail-Oriented Contributors:** Your meticulous nature ensures no task falls through the cracks, helping the team avoid careless errors.
- **Client-Facing Stars:** If your role involves interacting with clients or customers, your warmth and helpful nature will build trust and positive relationships.

Team Roles Where ESFJs Shine

ESFJs can excel in a variety of team roles, but often gravitate towards those that emphasize:

- **Facilitators:** Roles where you lead meetings, manage group discussions, and ensure everyone's voice is heard suit your natural ability to create inclusive spaces.
- **Organizers:** You thrive in roles requiring planning, project coordination, and ensuring the team meets deadlines and stays on track.
- **Support Specialists:** Whether it's customer service, administrative support, or human resources, your dedication to helping others succeed makes you a natural fit for support-oriented roles.
- **Trainers and Mentors:** Your patience, clear communication, and genuine desire to see others grow make you effective in roles where you guide and develop team members.

Potential Team Dynamics Challenges

While team-oriented, even ESFJs can face challenges in group work settings:

- **Dominant Personalities:** Outspoken or overly assertive teammates might inadvertently steamroll ESFJs, who prefer a more democratic group dynamic.
- **Unclear Roles:** Ambiguity about responsibilities can lead to frustration, as ESFJs thrive with defined tasks and expectations.
- **Lack of Appreciation:** If your behind-the-scenes contributions go unnoticed, it can lead to discouragement and a depletion of your natural enthusiasm.
- **Slow Decision-Making:** ESFJs sometimes struggle with teams that get stuck in analysis paralysis, preferring a more action-oriented approach.
- **Uncompromising Teammates:** Collaborating with inflexible individuals who are unwilling to budge from their position can clash with your desire for compromise and harmony.

Tips for Thriving in Teams

- **Communicate Your Needs:** Don't be afraid to speak up if you require clarification on tasks or feel overwhelmed by your workload.

- **Self-Advocate:** Subtly highlight your contributions during team meetings or updates to ensure your hard work is recognized.
- **Build Alliances:** Develop strong relationships with team members who value your perspective and are receptive to collaboration.
- **Set Boundaries with Demanding Teammates:** Learn to politely but firmly decline unreasonable requests or push back when your workload is unmanageable.
- **Focus on What You Can Control:** You can't change others' personalities. Focus on fulfilling your own tasks to the best of your ability and fostering positive relationships where possible.

Finding the Right Team Culture

Not all teams are created equal. Seek out workplaces with these traits that will support your success:

- **Emphasis on Collaboration:** Environments that prioritize teamwork and cooperation over individual ego and competition will be most fulfilling for you.
- **Appreciative Leadership:** Managers who actively recognize the contributions of all team members create a morale-boosting atmosphere for ESFJs.
- **Focus on Mission:** Feeling connected to the company's broader mission or purpose adds a layer of meaning to your day-to-day work.
- **Healthy Conflict Resolution:** Teams that have open channels for addressing disagreements in a constructive manner will minimize the disharmony that ESFJs find so draining.

ESFJs have the potential to make extraordinary contributions to any team. By understanding your strengths, navigating potential challenges, and seeking out collaborative and supportive environments, you can find a deep sense of fulfillment and belonging within your professional life.

CAREGIVING CAREERS: WHERE ESFJS SHINE BRIGHTEST

If there were a Hall of Fame for compassionate, dedicated caregivers, ESFJs would occupy the first wing. Your innate empathy, practical skills, and desire to make a tangible difference in people's lives make you uniquely suited for careers in the caregiving field. Let's explore some specific areas where your talents can truly shine.

Healthcare

- **Nursing:** Nurses, particularly in fields like pediatrics, geriatrics, or hospice care, play a vital role in providing patients with physical care and emotional support. Your bedside manner, attention to detail, and ability to advocate for patients would make you excel in this field.
- **Occupational or Physical Therapy:** Helping patients regain mobility, adapt to challenges, and improve their quality of life aligns perfectly with your supportive and encouraging nature.
- **Medical Assisting:** The diverse responsibilities, blending patient care and administrative support, suit your helpful and organized personality.
- **Social Work in Healthcare Settings:** Assisting patients and families in navigating complex medical systems, accessing resources, and coping with diagnoses taps into both your empathy and practical problem-solving skills.

Education & Development

- **Early Childhood Education:** Your nurturing instincts and love for creating fun, engaging environments make you an incredible asset in preschools, daycares, or as an elementary teacher.

- **Special Needs Support:** Working with children or adults with disabilities allows you to make a life-changing impact. Your patience, adaptability, and ability to celebrate small wins are essential in this field.
- **Counseling:** With further training, your empathy and desire to help others could lead to a fulfilling career as a school counselor, mental health counselor, or family therapist.

Community & Social Service

- **Non-Profit Work:** Organizations focused on causes you care about – homelessness, poverty, advocacy – benefit hugely from your dedication, organizational skills, and ability to connect with people from all walks of life.
- **Senior Care:** Whether assisted living, home care, or activity coordination, your ability to create a warm, supportive environment and bring joy to the lives of older adults is deeply meaningful.
- **Case Management:** Roles assisting vulnerable populations in navigating social services, finding housing, or accessing support align with your desire to help and provide practical solutions.

What Makes ESFJs Great Caregivers

- **Authentic Care:** Your empathy isn't just an act – it's the core of who you are. You genuinely care about the well-being of those you help.
- **Dedication and Responsibility:** You take commitments seriously and go above and beyond to ensure those you care for receive the best possible support.
- **Advocacy:** ESFJs are natural advocates, fighting for the needs of those who may not have a strong voice of their own.
- **Emotional Strength:** While deeply empathetic, you have a reservoir of inner strength that allows you to handle challenging situations with grace and resilience.
- **Practical Help:** You combine empathy with the drive to find practical solutions and improvements for those under your

care.

Considerations for Caregiving Careers

- **Emotional Burnout:** The most challenging aspect of caregiving is the potential for emotional exhaustion. Self-care and strong boundaries are essential.
- **Financial Compensation:** Caregiving roles, while incredibly important, aren't always highly paid. It's vital to find a balance between financial needs and fulfilling your calling.
- **Challenging Work:** Caregiving can be physically and emotionally demanding. Be realistic about your limits and seek support when needed.
- **The Rewards:** While not without challenges, nothing can replace the deep satisfaction of knowing you've made a genuine difference in someone's life.

Finding Your Caregiving Path

- **Identify Your Passion:** What populations are you most drawn to? Children, the elderly, those facing specific challenges?
- **Required Training:** Research the education and certifications needed for various caregiving roles to create a realistic plan.
- **Volunteer Experience:** Volunteering is a great way to test the waters, gain experience, and make connections in your desired field.
- **Network:** Connect with professionals working in caregiving roles to gain insider perspective and potential leads.

ESFJs born with a natural caregiving heart find immense fulfillment in these demanding yet deeply meaningful professions. If you feel the calling, let your empathy, compassion, and practicality lead the way to find a caregiving path that lights up both your heart and your life.

WHEN EMPATHY OVERWHELMS: MANAGING EMOTIONAL BURNOUT

ESFJs, your extraordinary empathy is a superpower, but like any superpower, it's crucial to learn how to manage it lest it becomes a vulnerability. Your sensitivity to others' emotions, combined with your relentless desire to help, can make you susceptible to emotional burnout. Let's understand this phenomenon and equip you with tools for prevention and recovery.

What is Emotional Burnout?

Emotional burnout is a state of chronic emotional and mental exhaustion often accompanied by feelings of cynicism, detachment, and reduced effectiveness. In the case of ESFJs, it often arises from these factors:

- **Empathic Overload:** Constantly absorbing the emotions of others can leave you feeling drained, as if you're carrying everyone else's burdens along with your own.
- **Neglecting Self-Care:** Putting everyone else's needs first leads to sacrificing your own physical and emotional well-being, depleting your internal resources.
- **Unrealistic Expectations:** The desire to always be there for everyone and solve their problems sets an impossible standard for yourself.
- **Bottling Up Emotions:** ESFJs may suppress their own feelings to maintain harmony, leading to an internal pressure cooker that eventually explodes.

Signs of Emotional Burnout

Don't wait until you hit a wall. Watch for these early signs:

- **Persistent Exhaustion:** Feeling chronically tired, even with enough sleep.
- **Emotional Sensitivity:** Increased irritability, tearfulness, or feeling emotionally overwhelmed by minor stressors.
- **Cynicism and Detachment:** Loss of joy in helping, feelings of apathy or disconnect from those you normally care about.
- **Decreased Effectiveness:** Feeling less competent at work or finding it hard to concentrate and make decisions.
- **Physical Symptoms:** Headaches, digestive issues, insomnia, or changes in appetite can be manifestations of emotional stress.
- **Isolation:** Withdrawing from social events and loved ones when what you need most is connection and support.

Prevention is Key

Cultivate these practices to build resilience and prevent burnout:

1. **Intentional Self-Care:**
- Schedule non-negotiable "me-time" for activities that recharge you—a calming bath, a walk in nature, or reading a good book.
- Prioritize sleep, healthy eating, and regular exercise. These are the foundations of emotional well-being.
- Learn mindfulness techniques to calm your mind and practice staying present instead of getting swept away by emotional undercurrents.
2. **Robust Boundaries:**
- Practice saying "no" tactfully but firmly without offering lengthy justifications or feeling guilty.
- Delegate tasks whenever possible, both at work and at home, to share the load.
- Set limits on how much time and emotional energy you invest in others' problems.
- Take breaks from emotionally heavy situations, even if it's just a few minutes to step outside and breathe deeply.
3. **Emotional Processing:**

- Schedule regular "worry time" to process concerns, then release them instead of dwelling on them all day.
- Journaling can be a powerful tool for expressing and understanding your emotions.
- Talking to a trusted friend, therapist, or counselor provides a safe space to vent, gain perspective, and receive support.

Strategies for Recovery

If you're already feeling burnt out, these steps help:

- **Take a Break:** If possible, request time off from work, scale back on responsibilities, or plan a relaxing escape where your primary focus is your own well-being.
- **Seek Support:** Don't try to go through this alone. Share your struggle with loved ones and consider professional therapy for tools and guidance.
- **Focus on the Basics:** Prioritize sleep, nourishing food, gentle movement, and activities that bring small sparks of joy.
- **Patience and Self-Compassion:** Recovery takes time. Be gentle with yourself and focus on small steps forward each day.

Remember: You Can't Pour from an Empty Cup

Caring for others is part of your nature, but it must be balanced with caring for yourself. See these practices not as selfish, but as the key to:

- **Sustainable Giving:** You can help others more effectively when you're emotionally balanced and well-resourced.
- **Role Modeling:** You teach others about healthy boundaries and self-care by example.
- **Protecting Your Gift:** Empathy is precious. Safeguard it to ensure you can continue using it to make the world a better place.

By recognizing the signs of burnout, prioritizing self-care, and seeking help when needed, you can manage your remarkable empathy. You'll not only protect yourself but thrive in the joy of helping others from a place of strength, not depletion.

THE NEED FOR HARMONY: DEALING WITH CONFLICT

ESFJs, with your strong desire for social harmony, find conflict inherently unsettling. Your natural inclination is to smooth things over, compromise, or even avoid difficult conversations altogether. While well-intentioned, this aversion can create long-term issues if left unchecked. Let's explore why conflict feels challenging and equip you with tools for addressing it constructively.

Why ESFJs Dislike Conflict

- **Empathy Overload:** You acutely feel the negative emotions of others during conflict, making the experience viscerally uncomfortable for you.
- **Harmony is Your Happy Place:** Disagreements disrupt the sense of connection and positivity you value so highly in your relationships.
- **Fear of Damaging Relationships:** You may worry that expressing conflicting opinions will cause others to dislike you or lead to a breakdown in the relationship.
- **People-Pleasing Tendencies:** You may sacrifice your own needs and opinions to avoid any perceived disapproval or upset from others.
- **Lack of Experience:** If you grew up in a conflict-avoidant environment, you likely haven't had the opportunity to develop healthy conflict resolution skills.

The Potential Dangers of Chronic Conflict Avoidance

While avoiding conflict offers temporary relief, it often leads to:

- **Buried Resentments:** Unexpressed frustrations fester, eroding trust and creating distance in the relationship.

- **Missed Opportunities for Growth:** Conflict, when navigated constructively, can be a catalyst for deeper understanding, positive change, and stronger bonds.
- **Imbalance of Power:** Chronically conceding to the other person creates a dynamic where your needs and opinions are consistently sidelined.
- **Increased Stress and Anxiety:** The worry about unspoken issues can create a constant low-level sense of unease.
- **Perpetuating the Pattern:** Conflict avoidance models unhealthy behavior to children or others who learn from your example.

Shifting Your Mindset about Conflict

- **Conflict is Natural:** Disagreement is a normal part of any relationship. It doesn't mean the relationship is failing.
- **Perspective is Key:** Try seeing conflict as an opportunity to understand another person better, find solutions, or strengthen the bond by working through a challenge together.
- **Respectful Disagreement is Possible:** You can express your opinions and needs firmly without resorting to aggression or personal attacks.

Tips for Approaching Conflict as an ESFJ

- **Timing is Important:** Don't try to have a difficult conversation when you're feeling emotionally overwhelmed or the other person is angry.
- **Start Small:** Practice expressing differences of opinion in low-stakes situations to build your confidence and skill set.
- **Focus on "I" Messages:** Instead of "You always...," frame things like, "I feel hurt when..." or "I would prefer it if ..."
- **Actively Listen:** Seek to truly understand the other person's perspective, even if you disagree. Look for points of common ground.
- **Compromise is a Win:** Focus on finding solutions that address the needs of both parties, even if it means neither

person gets 100% of what they want.

- **Take a Break if Needed:** If things get heated, it's okay to agree to take a break and resume the conversation when you're both calmer.
- **Don't Take Things Personally:** Separate the disagreement from your overall worth and the strength of the relationship.

When to Seek Outside Help:

- **Deeply Rooted Patterns:** If conflict avoidance stems from childhood experiences, professional therapy can help unpack those patterns and develop healthier responses.
- **High-Stakes Conflicts:** For major differences (in parenting styles, finances, etc.), a mediator can facilitate a fair and balanced conversation.
- **Abusive Situations:** Conflict resolution is NOT appropriate in relationships where there is emotional or physical abuse. Your safety is the priority.

Remember: Your Voice Matters

Learning to navigate conflict healthily is an act of self-love and empowerment. You have the right to express your needs, opinions, and set boundaries, even when it feels uncomfortable. By developing these skills, you'll gain confidence, foster more authentic relationships, and ultimately strengthen your ability to create the harmony you so deeply value.

THE POWER OF ROUTINE: FINDING STABILITY AND SECURITY

ESFJs find comfort and thrive in environments with structure and predictability. Routines, whether big or small, provide a sense of order and control, reducing anxiety and allowing you to focus your energy on the things that truly matter. Let's dive into the benefits of routines and how to create ones that work for you.

Why ESFJs Love Routine

- **Reduces Decision Fatigue:** Having established routines for daily tasks (meal planning, morning prep, etc.) frees up mental energy for more important or creative decisions.
- **Enhanced Efficiency:** When you have a system in place, tasks flow smoothly, minimizing wasted time and helping you accomplish more.
- **Stress Reduction:** Predictability creates a sense of security and reduces anxiety triggered by uncertainty or feeling overwhelmed.
- **Fosters Healthy Habits:** Routines make it easier to prioritize things like exercise, healthy eating, or self-care because they become ingrained in your schedule.
- **Supports Your "Helper" Nature:** Routines help you manage your household and responsibilities effectively, allowing you to better support the people you care for.

Types of Routines for ESFJs

- **Daily Life Routines:** Consistent morning and evening routines create bookends to your day, providing structure and predictability. These can include:
  - Wake-up time, bedtime, healthy breakfast choices

- Steps for getting ready for work or school
- Evening wind-down activities, like a warm bath, reading, or quiet time
- **Work Routines:** Established work processes help you stay organized, prioritize tasks, and minimize workplace stress. This might include:
  - Consistent ways to manage emails, schedule project steps, or organize files
  - Daily or weekly check-ins on long-term projects
- **Family Routines:** Routines with children provide stability and minimize power struggles. This includes clear expectations around:
  - Mealtimes, homework time, bedtime routines
  - Regular chores or responsibilities
  - Family time traditions (game nights, Sunday dinners, etc.)
- **Self-Care Routines:** Schedule specific activities that recharge you, whether it's a daily walk/workout, creative hobbies, or time for quiet reflection.

Tips for Creating Effective Routines

- **Start Small:** Don't try to overhaul everything at once. Focus on establishing one or two new routines at a time.
- **Flexibility is Key:** Allow some wiggle room within routines, as life can be unpredictable. The goal is a sense of flow, not rigidity.
- **Involve Others:** Get family members or colleagues on board with routines that affect them, encouraging input and finding solutions that work for everyone.
- **Written Plans Help:** Especially for complex routines, write down your steps to keep them consistent and make them easier to tweak for improvement.
- **Review and Adjust:** Routines aren't set in stone. Evaluate what's working and what's not, and make changes as needed to better fit your life.

Potential Pitfalls & Solutions

- **Boredom:** Prevent routines from becoming stagnant by adding some variation. Switch up meal plans, try a new workout, or change the scenery of your relaxation time.
- **Resistance from Others:** Kids, partners, or colleagues may resist new routines. Explain the benefits and get them involved to foster a sense of ownership.
- **Life Changes:** Adjust routines as needed when life circumstances shift – a new job, moving house, a baby, etc.
- **Unrealistic Expectations:** Avoid perfectionism when it comes to routines. Some days won't go exactly as planned, and that's okay.

The Beauty of Routine for ESFJs

While some personality types might feel stifled by routine, ESFJs find a unique freedom within it. Routines give you the foundation to:

- **Pursue Goals:** With everyday life running smoothly, you can focus on bigger goals, whether personal or professional.
- **Maximize Contribution:** You're free to offer your best as a helper and caregiver when basic needs and tasks are streamlined.
- **Be More Present:** When you're not plagued by decision fatigue or the stress of disorganization, you can be truly present with your loved ones.
- **Nurture Spontaneity:** Routines provide a baseline of security that allows you to occasionally embrace spontaneity and adventure without feeling destabilized.

Routines are a powerful tool in the ESFJ toolkit. By embracing the power of structured and predictable systems, you create a greater sense of calm, efficiency, and the capacity to live your life to the fullest.

PERFECTIONISM PITFALLS: EMBRACING "GOOD ENOUGH"

ESFJs, with your dedication to excellence and desire to create order, sometimes struggle with perfectionism. The pursuit of flawlessness can be both a strength, pushing you to high achievement, and a trap, leading to burnout, dissatisfaction, and unnecessary stress. Let's unpack this tendency and develop strategies for finding a healthier balance.

How Perfectionism Manifests in ESFJs

- **All-or-Nothing Thinking:** Projects or tasks are seen as either complete successes or utter failures, with little room for the middle ground.
- **Procrastination:** The fear of not doing something perfectly can lead to delaying or avoiding starting important tasks.
- **Setting Unrealistic Standards:** You expect perfection from yourself and others, setting a bar that is consistently out of reach.
- **Excessive Focus on Details:** Getting bogged down in minutiae slows progress and leads to missing the bigger picture.
- **Difficulty Delegating:** The belief that "If you want it done right, do it yourself" creates an unsustainable workload.
- **Harsh Self-Criticism:** Focusing intensely on mistakes or perceived shortcomings, eroding your self-confidence.

The Cost of Perfectionism

While striving for your best is admirable, chronic perfectionism has these consequences:

- **Increased Anxiety:** The constant pressure to be perfect fuels anxiety and a sense of never being good enough.

- **Missed Deadlines:** Projects stall due to overthinking, a refusal to submit work that's less than "perfect", and analysis paralysis.
- **Damaged Relationships:** Holding others to unrealistic standards creates tension in personal and professional relationships.
- **Diminished Joy:** You find it hard to celebrate accomplishments as you're always focused on what could have been better.
- **Burnout:** Perfectionism is exhausting. The relentless drive to be flawless is unsustainable and risks complete burnout.

Taming Your Perfectionist Tendencies

- **Challenge Your Thoughts:** Reframe "I must be perfect" to "I will try my best." Recognize that perfection is unattainable.
- **Focus on Progress Not Perfection:** Celebrate small wins and forward movement, even if things aren't flawless.
- **The 80/20 Rule:** For many tasks, getting it 80% right is good enough. Focus on the most essential aspects and let go of minor details.
- **Embrace Learning from Mistakes:** Mistakes are opportunities for growth, not signs of personal failure.
- **Practice Self-Compassion:** Speak to yourself with the same kindness you would extend to a friend. Acknowledge your effort even when you fall short of your own expectations.
- **Set Realistic Deadlines:** Break projects into smaller steps with achievable deadlines to prevent procrastination and overwhelm.
- **Delegate Strategically:** Identify tasks others can do, even if not exactly the way you would. Teach and trust others to help share the load.
- **Done is Better than Perfect:** Sometimes a completed project, even if imperfect, is infinitely better than no project at all.

The Gift of "Good Enough"

Striving for "good enough" may feel counterintuitive, but it leads to:

- **Greater Productivity:** You actually get more done when you release the need for perfection and focus on completion.
- **Reduced Stress:** Letting go of unattainable standards brings a greater sense of peace and reduces anxiety.
- **Healthy Risk-Taking:** You're more likely to try new things or take calculated risks without the fear of imperfect outcomes.
- **Increased Creativity:** Perfectionism stifles creativity. Embracing imperfection frees you up to experiment and try new approaches.
- **Stronger Relationships:** People feel less judged and more supported when you let go of expecting perfection from them.

Important Reminder: High Standards are NOT the Enemy

This chapter is not about lowering your standards or encouraging mediocrity. It's about distinguishing between:

- **Healthy Pursuit of Excellence:** Putting forth your best effort, taking pride in your work, and striving for growth.
- **Destructive Perfectionism:** Setting an unreasonably high bar, engaging in negative self-talk, and tying your worth to flawless results.

Finding a healthy balance will allow you to achieve great things without sacrificing your mental health and emotional well-being in the process.

BEYOND THE STEREOTYPE: UNLOCKING ESFJ INDIVIDUALITY

ESFJs are often characterized by their warmth, practicality, and social skills. Yet, it's important to remember that, like any personality type, there's far more than meets the eye. This chapter is about embracing the unique nuances that make you, well...you!

Challenging the "Caretaker" Mold

While caring for others is part of your nature, it doesn't define your entire identity. Here's how to break free from limiting stereotypes:

- **Explore Your Hobbies:** Pursue interests that are purely for your own enjoyment—creative expression, learning a new skill, competitive sports, whatever lights you up.
- **Surprise People:** Occasionally make choices based on what YOU want, even if it runs counter to what others expect from helpful, agreeable you.
- **Develop Unrelated Expertise:** Become the go-to person for a topic completely outside of your "caretaker" domain – tech genius, financial guru, history buff – surprising people with your breadth of knowledge.
- **Embrace the "Unhelpful" Day:** Once in a while, declare a day where you do only the absolute minimum for others. This radical self-care is essential.

Developing Your Introverted Sensing (Si)

Your auxiliary function, Introverted Sensing, connects you to past experiences, detail, and tradition. Cultivating this side of you adds depth:

- **Honor Your History:** Create a family scrapbook, take up genealogy, or preserve meaningful traditions. This honors your past and brings richness to the present.

- **The Joy of Memory:** Recall specific sensory details of past experiences (sights, smells, sounds). This connects you to the richness of your life.
- **Tried and True:** Find comfort and pleasure in repeating experiences you enjoy - a favorite restaurant, rereading a book, revisiting a meaningful location.
- **Systems and Routines:** Your love of order is Si at work! Lean into finding new areas where systems bring you efficiency and pleasure.

Nurturing Your Ne (Extraverted Intuition)

Your tertiary function, Extraverted Intuition, is your connection to possibilities and brainstorming. Nurturing this adds a touch of playfulness:

- **The "What If?" Game:** Embrace playful brainstorming about anything - crazy business ideas, alternate histories, fantastical scenarios.
- **Change It Up:** Try new things just for the sake of novelty, stepping a little outside your comfort zone. Order a new dish, take a scenic route home.
- **Embrace Play:** Engage in activities that encourage free-flowing imagination – improvisation, charades, imaginative play with kids.
- **Follow Your Curiosity:** When something sparks your interest, even if random or impractical, explore it! A short online course, a documentary, a new hobby.

The Power of Your Ti (Introverted Thinking)

Your inferior function, Introverted Thinking, represents logic and internal reasoning. This is your least developed area, but flexing it brings balance:

- **Be a Skeptic:** Question assumptions, look for inconsistencies in arguments, and seek logical proof before adopting an opinion.

- **Problem Puzzle:** Enjoy brain teasers, logic games, or tackling complex problems that require analyzing facts and step-by-step reasoning.
- **Debate Club:** Engage in respectful debates on topics you're passionate about. This hones your ability to construct and defend logical arguments.
- **Efficiency Engineer:** Look for ways to streamline processes, maximize systems, and eliminate unnecessary steps in both work and personal tasks.

The Beauty of the Individual ESFJ

ESFJ warmth and caregiving are truly gifts to the world. But remember:

- **You Are Not One-Dimensional:** Your personality is multifaceted. Embrace your unique interests, talents, and quirky habits.
- **Growth is Lifelong:** Actively developing less dominant aspects of your personality adds richness, resilience, and keeps things interesting.
- **There's No "Right" Way to Be an ESFJ:** Authenticity means embracing the full spectrum of who you are, both the expected strengths and the unexpected quirks.

By challenging stereotypes, nurturing less familiar parts of your personality, and embracing your inherent individuality, you become the fullest, most vibrant version of your wonderful ESFJ self.

INTROVERTED FEELING: UNDERSTANDING YOUR INNER COMPASS

While Extraverted Feeling (Fe) is your dominant decision-making powerhouse, your inferior function, Introverted Feeling (Fi), plays a subtle yet important role in your inner world. Understanding Fi helps you gain better self-awareness and make choices that honor your most deeply held values.

How Introverted Feeling Works

Fi is focused on internal authenticity and deeply held personal convictions. Unlike Fe, which prioritizes external harmony, Fi asks:

- **What truly matters to me?:** Fi helps you identify your core values, the things that give your life meaning and purpose.
- **Am I being true to myself?:** Fi acts as your moral compass, nudging you when your actions feel incongruent with your beliefs.
- **What feels right to me?** Fi influences gut instincts and subtle preferences, even when you can't clearly articulate the reasons.
- **Does this align with my identity?:** Fi helps you define who you are at your core and make choices that feel authentic to that identity.

Immature vs. Developed Fi

As your least developed function, Fi can manifest in a few less-than-ideal ways early on:

- **Unexamined Values:** You might operate from absorbed values (family, society, etc.) without consciously deciding if they're truly yours.

- **Black-and-White Thinking:** Strong "this is right/wrong" stances without the nuance gained from more developed Fi.
- **Difficulty Expressing Fi:** You struggle to put your feelings or core convictions into words, as Fe is your more dominant form of expression.
- **Unintentional Harshness:** Fi-based opinions sometimes come out bluntly due to lack of Fe's softening filters.

Nurturing Your Introverted Feeling

Here's how to strengthen your Fi muscle and integrate it healthily:

1. **Values Exploration:**
- Identify your top 5 core values (honesty, kindness, ambition, etc.).
- Reflect on past choices: Where did you feel most aligned/ misaligned with your values? Why?
- Journal about situations where you felt a strong internal "yes" or "no" even if the logical reasons weren't clear.
2. **Practice Articulating Fi:**
- Start with small opinions: Explain to someone why you prefer a certain type of music, food, or movie. Focus on the feeling beneath the preference.
- Learn Fi-based vocabulary: Words like "authentic," "meaningful," "integrity," and "congruent" can help communicate your inner world.
- Talk to a trusted friend: Share deeper convictions and seek their feedback on how clearly you express your Fi perspective.
3. **Fi Decision-Making:**
- Consciously use Fi alongside Fe: When a decision triggers both Fe (what will make others happy) and Fi (what feels right to me), listen to both sides.
- Start with low-stakes decisions: Use Fi to choose things based purely on personal preference, even if they have minor social consequences.

- Embrace complexity: Fi helps you see the gray areas where 'right' and 'wrong' aren't always clear-cut.

Fi as a Source of Strength for ESFJs

A developed Fi grants you:

- **Greater Self-Awareness:** You understand your motivations, what matters most to you, and why certain situations feel draining even when outwardly they seem "fine."
- **Integrity:** Strong Fi helps you resist people-pleasing when it clashes with your core values.
- **Grounded Confidence:** Knowing and living in alignment with your values creates inner peace that is less reliant on external validation.
- **Healthy Boundaries:** Fi fuels the ability to say a firm "no" to protect your energy and priorities when something violates your deepest convictions.
- **Nuanced Empathy:** Understanding your own values deepens your capacity to understand and respect values different from your own.

Remember:

- **Fi Takes Time:** Be patient with yourself. Introverted functions usually develop more fully in mid-life and beyond.
- **It's a Complement, Not a Replacement:** Healthy Fi integrates with your dominant Fe, creating a richer and more balanced decision-making toolkit.

By paying attention to those moments your internal compass tugs you in certain directions, you unlock a deeper layer of authenticity and personal conviction. This strengthens you as you navigate the complex, nuanced, value-laden choices that life will inevitably bring your way.

EXTRAVERTED SENSING: ENGAGING WITH THE WORLD

ESFJs, though primarily focused on the world of people and social dynamics, also possess Extraverted Sensing (Se). This function is your connection to the concrete, present moment, and the enjoyment of tangible experiences. Developing your Se brings balance to your life and opens up new avenues for fun and personal growth.

How Extraverted Sensing Shows Up for ESFJs

While not your dominant mode, Se manifests in several ways:

- **Appreciation for the Physical World:** You may enjoy beautiful surroundings, nature, comfortable furniture, and visually appealing presentations of food or décor.
- **Drawn to Action:** Sometimes sitting and pondering feels less satisfying than actively doing. You learn best through hands-on experience.
- **Aesthetics Matter:** You have an eye for details and take pride in making your home, workspace, or even your appearance neat and appealing.
- **Occasional Adrenaline Junkie:** While usually cautious, you might have a slightly daredevilish side that enjoys a bit of thrill – fast rides, lively sporting events, or trying adventurous new foods.

The Challenges of Underdeveloped Se

ESFJs risk overlooking Se, but this limits you in a few ways:

- **Overthinking and Missing the Moment:** Anxious thoughts about the future or rumination on past issues can prevent you from fully enjoying the present.
- **Getting Stuck in Routines:** A strong Si focus on routine and

tradition can make life feel predictable. Se helps you inject spontaneity and freshness.

- **Missing Out on Simple Pleasures:** Overemphasis on others can lead to neglecting your own needs for sensory enjoyment and physical experiences.
- **Dislike of Unexpected Changes:** Unplanned disruptions can feel unsettling. Developing Se enhances your adaptability and openness to the unexpected.

Tips for Cultivating Your Extraverted Sensing

Embrace the here and now with these practices:

- **Engage Your Senses:** Pay attention to the details – sights, smells, textures, sounds. Savor delicious food, appreciate the beauty of nature, or get lost in a piece of music.
- **Get Moving:** Engage in physical activities you enjoy – dance, sports, gardening, even a brisk walk. Tune in to the sensations in your body.
- **Spontaneous Adventures:** Break from routine with an unplanned outing – try a new restaurant, explore a local park, or sign up for a last-minute class.
- **Embrace Novelty:** Seek out new experiences – travel to a new place, try an exotic cuisine, or learn a hands-on skill like painting or woodworking.
- **Mindfulness Practices:** Ground yourself in the present moment through meditation, yoga, or focused breathing exercises to combat overthinking.

Benefits of Embracing Se

- **Stress Reduction:** Focusing on the present through sensory experiences offers a mental break from worries and allows you to recharge.
- **Increased Joy and Appreciation:** You discover and savor the simple pleasures of life, finding joy in everyday experiences.
- **Adaptability:** Strengthening Se helps you roll with the punches and embrace changes in your environment with

greater ease.

- **Creativity Boost:** Sensory experiences often spark fresh ideas and fuel creative expression, whether through hobbies or your work.
- **Enhanced Social Life:** Se helps you be more fully present with others, creating deeper connections and more engaging interactions.

Se as a Superpower

Your natural focus on people and social harmony is an incredible strength, but don't forget:

- **Balance is Key:** Integrating Se creates a fuller, more well-rounded life experience and helps combat some of your natural tendencies towards worry.
- **Simple = Powerful:** Se reminds you that joy can be found in the most basic experiences, which fosters contentment and gratitude.
- **Presence is a Gift:** The ability to fully inhabit the present moment makes you a better friend, partner, and parent.

By consciously seeking out experiences that engage your senses, you'll open yourself up to new possibilities for fun, growth, and greater overall life satisfaction. Your adventurous spirit has always been there waiting – let your Extraverted Sensing show you the way!

THE ESFJ SHADOW: EXPLORING HIDDEN DEPTHS

Like every personality type, ESFJs have a "shadow side." This isn't about being "bad" but rather about the less developed or unconscious aspects of your personality, hidden from typical daily awareness. Understanding your shadow offers potential for tremendous growth, balance, and even reveals untapped talents.

Key Shadow Functions for ESFJs

While all cognitive functions can have shadow expressions, the most important for ESFJs are those opposing your dominant and auxiliary:

- **Introverted Thinking (Ti):** If your dominant Fe prioritizes social harmony and external values, your shadow Ti represents a hidden critical streak. This often surfaces as unexpressed frustrations turned inward, harshly judging yourself according to your own internal logic.
- **Extraverted Intuition (Ne):** With Si as your comfort zone (tradition, details), your shadow Ne holds unexplored possibilities. This side of you might express as occasional bursts of scattered ideas, fears of the unknown, or a sense of being trapped by routines.
- **Introverted Sensing (Si):** While Si offers comfort in the familiar, its shadow can manifest as resistance to any change, an overemphasis on details at the expense of the bigger picture, or clinging to outdated traditions even when they no longer serve.
- **Extraverted Feeling (Fe):** Ironically, even warm ESFJs can have a shadow Fe. This manifests as extreme sensitivity to even subtle disapproval, reading negativity where none is intended, or occasionally using emotional manipulation to

maintain a sense of control in relationships.

How the Shadow Surfaces

Your shadow side isn't lurking constantly. It typically surfaces in these ways:

- **Under Stress:** When overwhelmed or burnt out, you're less able to access your usual Fe warmth. You might become overly critical, fixate on small details, or withdraw emotionally.
- **Conflict:** Disagreements can trigger shadow Fe, leading to subtle manipulation or overreactions based on your fear of others' negative judgment.
- **Projections:** You might unconsciously project shadow qualities onto others. Frustration with someone's seemingly illogical choices (Ti) or lack of focus on details (Si) could reflect your own unintegrated aspects.
- **Unexpected Attraction:** Fascination with people who embody your shadow functions hints at your need for internal development. Wild impulsivity (Ne) or bluntness (Ti) might seem oddly appealing because they're so unfamiliar to you.

Embracing the Shadow for Growth

Understanding your shadow isn't about self-shaming, but an opportunity:

1. **Non-Judgmental Observation:** Notice when shadow tendencies arise (sharp inner critic, fears of change). Observe them curiously, not with guilt.
2. **Seek the Positive Intent:** Even shadow expressions have origins in trying to serve you. Fear of the unknown is a twisted form of self-protection.
3. **Safe Expression:** Journal, talk to a trusted friend, or find creative outlets to express shadow energy in a healthy way. Blowing off steam with dark humor or venting your inner critic privately prevents it from spilling into relationships.

4.   **Integrate Gradually:** Actively develop your weaker functions (Ti, Ne) in safe doses to counterbalance the pull of the shadow. Read a book on logic, try a brainstorming exercise, or experiment with small changes to create healthier expressions.

The Benefits of Shadow Work

- **Self-Compassion:** Understanding you have both sunny and shadow aspects lessens harsh self-judgment, increases resilience, and strengthens your core sense of worth.
- **Improved Relationships:** Recognizing shadow projections makes you less reactive to others, leading to fairer and more empathetic interactions.
- **Unlock Hidden Potential:** The shadow often holds untapped talents. Exploring your inner critic (Ti) might reveal skills in analysis, your fear of change (Si) could hide a need for more stability in your life.
- **Wholeness:** Embracing both your radiant strengths and your less-developed aspects creates a more integrated, authentic, and ultimately powerful sense of self.

Remember:

- **Shadow = Unconscious:** These aspects aren't intentional or malicious, but rather uncharted territory within your psyche.
- **Slow & Steady Wins:** Shadow work is lifelong. Small steps, focused on understanding not eradicating, lead to the most sustainable growth.

The journey into your shadow side may feel uncomfortable at times, but the rewards are great. By facing these hidden depths with bravery and self-compassion, you will illuminate the full spectrum of your being and become a more multifaceted, balanced, and truly remarkable ESFJ.

FAMOUS ESFJS: INSPIRATION FROM HISTORY AND POP CULTURE

Recognizing shared traits in known ESFJs offers a fascinating glimpse into the diverse ways your personality type manifests in the world. From historical figures to pop culture icons, these examples can inspire you to embrace your strengths and recognize both the bright and shadow sides of your ESFJ nature.

Historical Figures

- **Lyndon B. Johnson (US President):** Known for his warmth and people skills, yet his presidency's legacy includes escalation in Vietnam, demonstrating how strong Fe, without counterbalancing forces, can lead to people-pleasing decisions at the expense of the bigger picture.
- **Mother Teresa:** The epitome of ESFJ compassion, her tireless work for the poor showcases extraordinary empathy and self-sacrifice. She also offers a cautionary tale about the need for boundaries and avoiding glorifying burnout.
- **Princess Diana:** Dubbed "The People's Princess," Diana's genuine warmth and championing social causes resonate with the ESFJ spirit. Her struggles with boundaries and vulnerability to public opinion point to common ESFJ pitfalls.
- **Jimmy Carter (US President):** Exemplifies ESFJ sincerity and commitment to service. His focus on human rights demonstrates Fi-driven values, while some presidency struggles reveal potential downsides of leading with Fe over less-developed Ti logic.

Fictional Characters

- **Monica Geller (Friends):** Monica's love of hosting, organization, and slightly bossy helpfulness scream ESFJ. Her perfectionism and occasional overreactions in messy social situations offer relatable humor with a touch of ESFJ shadow.
- **Molly Weasley (Harry Potter):** The fiercely protective, nurturing matriarch of the Weasley clan is a classic ESFJ. Her occasional focus on tradition over flexibility (Si dominance) offers a lighthearted reminder of potential pitfalls.
- **Charlotte York Goldenblatt (Sex and the City):** Charlotte's commitment to finding love, her dedication to friendship, and adherence to social norms are ESFJ traits. Yet, her journey showcases struggles with self-worth tied to external validation.
- **Steve Rogers/Captain America (Marvel):** Steve's unwavering moral compass (Fi), loyalty to his team, and focus on protecting others embody the best of the ESFJ. His occasional struggles with adapting to change and seeing shades of gray reflect underdeveloped Se and Ti functions.

Pop Culture Icons

- **Taylor Swift:** Her early music's themes of belonging and social dynamics resonated strongly with ESFJs. Her evolution into a savvy businesswoman and outspoken advocate demonstrate the hidden strength and potential for Ti development.
- **Jennifer Garner:** Often playing relatable, kind characters, Garner herself reflects the ESFJ's warmth. Her dedication to family life and social causes highlights the ESFJ's ability to have both private and public impact.
- **Reese Witherspoon:** Her sunshine personality and entrepreneurial spirit reflect ESFJ warmth and practicality. Her drive to increase female representation in media highlights the power of values-guided action (Fi).
- **Chris Evans:** Exudes down-to-earth, helpful ESFJ energy. His

commitment to social causes, close family bonds, and ability to poke fun at himself show the balance of strong values and genuine approachability.

Key Takeaways

What can we learn from studying these diverse ESFJs?

- **Strengths as Double-Edged Swords:** Warmth can devolve into people-pleasing, a focus on order can become perfectionism. Your biggest assets also hold potential for the shadow.
- **Values Matter:** Many ESFJs use their Fe-powered social awareness to fight for deeply held causes, showcasing Fi-fueled convictions.
- **Growth is Possible:** Characters like Taylor Swift demonstrate how even with dominant Fe, ESFJs can learn to prioritize authenticity and stand up for what they believe in.
- **Balance is Key:** Fictional ESFJs often struggle at extremes – overly rigid or easily swayed by emotions. Finding healthy integration of all functions is crucial.

Important Note: Personalities are complex. While typing these figures can be a fun exercise, real people are never reducible to four letters.

Observing ESFJ traits in action helps you to:

- **Appreciate the Diversity within the Type:** ESFJs can be politicians, caregivers, pop stars, or your beloved aunt. The core functions manifest in unique ways.
- **Find Role Models:** Seek inspiration from figures who embody the qualities you wish to cultivate, whether kindness, advocacy, or creative expression.
- **Embrace Your Full Potential:** Recognizing common struggles alongside strengths provides a roadmap for your own personal growth journey.

As an ESFJ, you have the power to make a tremendous positive impact on the world. Let the examples of real and fictional ESFJs illuminate the path, reminding you that you're in very good company!

TIPS FOR LOVED ONES: SUPPORTING THE ESFJ IN YOUR LIFE

If you have an ESFJ in your life, you already know what a treasure they are! Their warmth, loyalty, and practical support enrich relationships of all kinds. To make the most of your connection, understanding their unique needs and challenges is key. Here's a guide for partners, family, friends, and colleagues on how to best love and support your ESFJ.

Appreciating Their Gifts

- **Acknowledge Their Effort:** ESFJs tirelessly work to make life better for those they care about. Express genuine gratitude for everything they do, big and small. Don't take their contributions for granted!
- **Celebrate Their Warmth:** ESFJs have huge hearts. Tell them how much their kindness, encouragement, and presence mean to you.
- **Value Their Practical Help:** Whether it's organizing a chaotic kitchen or remembering everyone's birthdays, ESFJs love being useful. Thank them for the ways they make things run smoothly.

Understanding Their Needs

- **Reciprocation is Vital:** ESFJs give a lot. Ensure you're making them feel loved, appreciated, and supported in return.
- **Words of Affirmation Matter:** They may not readily ask for it, but ESFJs crave validation and reassurance that their efforts are noticed and valued.
- **Emotional Sensitivity:** ESFJs are deeply empathetic. Be mindful of harsh criticism or disharmony, as they

internalize it even if it's not directed at them.

- **Alone Time for Recharging:** All that focus on others can be draining. Encourage them to take time for themselves, and respect their need for moments of solitude.

Navigating Potential Challenges

- **People-Pleasing Tendencies:** Help them set healthy boundaries. Remind them it's okay to say "no" and that their needs are equally important.
- **Sensitivity to Criticism:** Approach feedback gently, focusing on positives first. Frame it as an opportunity for growth, not a personal attack.
- **Perfectionism Pitfalls:** Encourage them to embrace "good enough" and celebrate progress instead of relentlessly striving for the unattainable.
- **Need for Routine:** Support their need for structure, while gently encouraging flexibility when plans need to change.

How to Show Love in Ways They'll Truly Feel

- **Quality Time:** Undivided attention is one of the most powerful gifts for an ESFJ. Put the phone away and be fully present in a conversation.
- **Acts of Service:** Pitch in with household tasks, take care of something they've been putting off, or surprise them with a thoughtful, practical gift.
- **Small Gestures with Big Impact:** A handwritten note of appreciation, remembering a meaningful date, or taking care of errands for them demonstrates deep understanding.
- **Plan Fun Outings:** ESFJs often put the needs of others first. Take initiative and plan a delightful experience tailored to their interests.
- **Physical Touch:** If appropriate to your relationship, hugs, holding hands, or a comforting back rub are deeply appreciated by ESFJs.

Additional Tips for Specific Relationships

- **Romantic Partners:** Prioritize intimacy, be emotionally expressive, and don't underestimate the power of romantic gestures, however small.
- **Friends:** Be a reliable confidant, cheer them on enthusiastically, and initiate plans, as they might prioritize your needs over making social overtures themselves.
- **Children:** Provide structure and clear expectations, create special family traditions, and openly express your love and pride for them.
- **Colleagues:** Show appreciation for their contributions to the team, acknowledge their dedication, and create a harmonious, collaborative atmosphere.

The Importance of Supporting ESFJ Growth

- **Encourage Exploration of Hobbies:** Help them carve out time for interests that are purely for their own enjoyment, not about serving others.
- **Develop Introverted Functions:** Gently push them outside their comfort zone, encouraging small doses of spontaneity (Ne) and the use of logic alongside their feelings (Ti).
- **Celebrate Self-Care:** Remind them that taking care of themselves isn't selfish, but rather allows them to give even more to others.

ESFJs bring warmth, joy, and unwavering support into the lives of those they love. By understanding their unique strengths, respecting their sensitivities, and actively showing your appreciation, you nurture a deep and fulfilling bond. Your efforts to support the ESFJ in your life will be rewarded tenfold by their love, loyalty, and the radiant light they bring into your world.

SELF-CARE ESSENTIALS FOR ESFJS: REPLENISHING YOUR ENERGY

ESFJs, your heart for helping others is boundless, but even the most dedicated caregivers need to replenish their own well of energy. Self-care isn't selfish, it's the key to sustaining your ability to give. This chapter offers a toolkit of practical strategies to prioritize your physical, emotional, and mental well-being, so you can thrive while continuing to make the world a better place.

Why Self-Care is Especially Crucial for ESFJs

1. **People-Pleasing Trap:** Your deep-seated desire to be helpful can lead to putting everyone else's needs first, depleting your own resources. Self-care teaches you boundaries.
2. **Empathy Overload:** Constantly absorbing the emotions of others leaves you emotionally drained. You must actively create space for processing and restoration.
3. **Perfectionism = Burnout:** Self-care is preventative medicine. Taking breaks, celebrating small wins, and embracing imperfections protects you from chronic exhaustion.
4. **Role Modeling:** Setting a good example for children, partners, or colleagues involves demonstrating that caring for yourself matters too.

Types of Self-Care

- **Physical Self-Care:**
  - **Sleep is Sacred:** Aim for 7-8 hours consistently. A regular sleep schedule allows you to recharge fully each day.
  - **Nourishing Food:** Your on-the-go life might lead to quick, unhealthy meals. Focus on whole foods, regular

meal times, and hydration.

- o **Movement You Enjoy:** Don't force yourself to exercise in ways you hate. Find activities that feel good – walking, dancing, a yoga class.
- o **Restorative Practices:** Warm baths, gentle stretching, or listening to calming music soothe your nervous system and promote relaxation.
- **Emotional Self-Care:**
  - o **Feel Your Feelings:** Schedule brief "worry time" to process anxieties, then consciously release them. Don't dwell 24/7.
  - o **Journaling:** Writing helps untangle emotions and brings clarity. Re-reading entries over time reveals patterns and progress.
  - o **Safe Space to Vent:** Have a trusted person you can confide in when overwhelmed, offering release and support.
  - o **Therapy is a Strength:** If you struggle with chronic anxiety or burnout, professional help equips you with coping tools and deepens self-understanding.
  - o **Fun as Medicine:** Injecting lightheartedness, laughter, and playfulness into your day combats stress and uplifts your mood.
- **Mental Self-Care**
  - o **Tech Timeouts:** Schedule breaks from social media, news, and screens in general. Your mind needs moments of unstimulated quiet.
  - o **Mindfulness Practices:** Simple meditation, even for 5 minutes, reduces mental chatter and brings presence to the here and now.
  - o **Boundary Bootcamp:** Practice saying "no" confidently to low-priority requests. Schedule time for your own needs without guilt.
  - o **Positive Self-Talk:** Counteract your inner critic with deliberate affirmations of your strengths and accomplishments.

Tips for Making Self-Care a Habit

- **Start Small:** Choose ONE new practice to implement this week. Tiny changes create momentum.
- **Schedule It:** Block off non-negotiable "me time" on your calendar like any other important appointment.
- **Ask for Support:** Let family/partners know you're working on self-care, so they can respect boundaries and offer help with household tasks.
- **Guilt-Busting Mindset:** Remind yourself that filling your own cup allows you to give more sustainably to others.

Self-Care Isn't One-Size-Fits-All!

Explore and find what TRULY feels rejuvenating for you:

- **Nature Immersion:** Time in green spaces reduces stress.
- **Creative Expression:** Any activity using your hands or imagination is therapeutic (drawing, baking, music, DIY projects).
- **Alone Time:** If you're always surrounded by people, solitude might be the most luxurious form of self-care.
- **Spiritual Practices:** If faith is important, nurture your spiritual side through prayer, services, or reflective readings.

Remember:

- **Consistency is Key:** Short, frequent self-care is better than occasional long splurges followed by neglect.
- **Listen to Your Body:** Each day, tune in. Do you need activity, rest, emotional processing? Honor those signals.
- **Don't Give Up!:** Some days will be better than others. Be kind to yourself as you create new patterns.

ESFJ, your boundless compassion for others is an incredible gift. Ensure that gift keeps shining brightly by making self-care a non-negotiable priority. Treat yourself with the same love and attention you so freely shower upon the world.

GROWTH MINDSET: DEVELOPING UNUSED STRENGTHS

ESFJs, understanding your dominant functions (Fe and Si) is important, but true growth and fulfillment often lie in developing those less familiar parts of your personality. Embracing a growth mindset allows you to access new strengths, improve existing skills, and create a more multifaceted, balanced sense of self. This chapter focuses on cultivating your tertiary (Ne) and inferior (Ti) functions.

Nurturing Ne (Extraverted Intuition)

Ne helps you see possibilities, brainstorm solutions, and embrace change. Developing Ne grants you:

- **Problem-Solving Boost:** Ne adds a creative dimension to your practical Fe skills. You'll see a wider array of potential solutions.
- **Reduced Fear of the Unknown:** Embracing Ne helps you adapt more easily to change and feel less threatened by uncertainty
- **Mental Agility:** Ne exercises your "idea muscles," keeping you flexible and preventing stagnation in your thinking.
- **Sparks of Inspiration:** You'll be surprised by the fun, creative ideas that emerge when you give Ne a bit of free rein.

How to Develop Your Ne

- **Brainstorming Sessions:** Alone or with others, generate ideas without judgment. Focus on quantity, not quality at first.
- **"What If...?" Game:** Challenge assumptions and play with possibilities. "What if I took a different career path?" "What if

I traveled for a year?"

- **Try New Things:** Expose yourself to novel experiences – a new cuisine, artistic medium, travel destination. Pay attention to what excites you.
- **Embrace Learning:** Take a class on a topic outside your comfort zone. The exploration itself is as valuable as the knowledge gained.

Developing Ti (Introverted Thinking)

Ti is about internal logic and analysis. Strengthening Ti helps you:

- **Set Stronger Boundaries:** Ti aids in spotting inconsistencies that help you say "no" with confidence when things don't align with your values.
- **Balance Heart and Head:** Ti helps temper overly emotional reactions with logical reasoning, leading to fairer decision-making.
- **Enhance Critical Thinking Skills:** Better Ti allows you to analyze situations more objectively, improving problem-solving in all areas.
- **Find Your Inner Authority:** A clearer sense of your own internal logic makes you less susceptible to the sway of external opinions.

How to Develop Your Ti

- **Socratic Questioning:** Ask yourself probing questions: "Why do I believe that?" "What evidence supports this idea?"
- **Debate for Fun:** Respectfully discuss topics you care about, focusing on constructing logical arguments, not winning.
- **Analyze Your Decisions:** After a choice, break down your reasoning process. Was it driven by Fe, Fi, or Ti? This builds self-awareness.
- **Logic Puzzles & Games:** Engage your Ti with Sudoku, crosswords, or even strategy-based video games.

Tips for a Successful Growth Journey

- **Patience is Key:** Developing your weaker functions takes time and consistent effort. Don't get discouraged by slow progress. .
- **Embrace Discomfort:** Leaning into your less-developed sides will feel awkward at first. That's a sign you're stretching beyond your comfort zone!
- **Start Small:** Choose one or two practices from the suggestions above. Don't attempt a personality overhaul overnight.
- **Playful Exploration:** Treat this as an adventure of self-discovery, keeping it lighthearted rather than self-critical.
- **Celebrate Victories:** Acknowledge those moments when you access Ne's creativity or Ti's logic, even in small ways. Positive reinforcement matters!

Important Reminders

- **You're Not Becoming a Different Type:** This is about enriching your existing strengths, not changing who you are at your core.
- **Fe and Si Are Still Awesome:** Your warmth and practicality are superpowers! You're simply adding new tools to your psychological toolkit.

ESFJ, by embracing a growth mindset and consciously nurturing your less-dominant functions, you'll unlock new potentials, overcome common challenges, and become the most dynamic, well-rounded version of yourself. Remember, growth is a lifelong adventure - enjoy the journey!

THE PATH FORWARD: EMBRACING YOUR ESFJ JOURNEY

ESFJ, understanding your personality type is more than just a label, it's a starting point for an incredible journey of self-discovery and personal growth. This final chapter offers reflections and guidance as you embrace all that it means to be a warm, nurturing, and practical Extraverted Feeling Judging type.

Lessons from Your Exploration

Take a moment to look back on the chapters you've read. Consider:

- **Major Revelations:** What surprised you most (positively or negatively) about being an ESFJ? Have any chapters radically altered your self-perception?
- **"Aha!" Moments:** Which insights about your strengths and struggles resonated the most? Are there specific patterns now clearer to you?
- **Actionable Takeaways:** Are there chapters that motivated you to make changes – prioritizing self-care, setting better boundaries, exploring new hobbies?

Facing Your Challenges with Compassion

ESFJ, it's easy to love your strengths. Facing challenges is the tougher part of growth. Remember:

- **Perfectionism is Not the Goal:** "Good enough" really IS good enough. The key is identifying what truly matters, and letting go of the rest.
- **Boundaries are Born of Self-Love:** Saying "no" doesn't make you less of a helper, it makes you a more sustainable helper.
- **The Shadow Isn't the Enemy:** Understanding those hidden

parts leads to greater self-compassion and awareness when they surface.

- **Seek Support When Needed:** You don't have to bear all your burdens alone. Friends, family, a therapist, or even a supportive online ESFJ community can help.

Celebrating Your Core Strengths

Never lose sight of the incredible qualities you possess as an ESFJ:

- **Emotional Intelligence Master:** Tap into your empathy as a superpower for understanding and connecting with others on a profound level.
- **Community Catalyst:** Use your social skills to bring people together, foster a sense of belonging, and create positive change in your world.
- **Practical Problem-Solver:** Turn caring into action. Channel your problem-solving prowess to improve situations for those around you.
- **Tradition Torchbearer:** Honor the importance of rituals, celebrations, and shared history as they bring meaning and connection.

The Beauty of Your Ongoing Evolution

Your personality, like you, is constantly evolving. Here's how to keep your growth mindset strong:

- Read (and Re-Read!): Return to chapters that resonated most when you need a reminder or a boost of self-understanding.
- **Observe Yourself in Action:** Notice when you're embodying your best qualities and where your ESFJ challenges tend to trip you up.
- **Community Connections:** Find like-minded ESFJs (online or in real life) for support, celebration, and sharing insights specific to your type.
- **One Step at a Time:** Personal growth is a marathon, not a sprint. Keep celebrating those small steps forward.

Your Guiding Light: Values

When overwhelmed, unsure, or facing major decisions, let your Fi compass guide you:

- **Know Your Core Few:** What 3-5 values are non-negotiable for you? Kindness, loyalty, family, integrity? Let these be your north star.
- **Values Check-In:** Before taking action, ask, "Does this align with what I believe truly matters most?"
- **Value Your Values:** Don't let Fe's desire for harmony make you compromise on what's essential to your personal sense of integrity.

The Legacy You'll Leave

ESFJ, the world needs your warmth, your connective spirit, and your unwavering belief in the power of human goodness. Through your actions, both large and small, you'll leave behind:

- **Countless Lives Touched:** People felt seen, understood, and supported because of you.
- **Stronger Communities:** You brought people together, creating friendships, networks, and a greater sense of belonging.
- **Ripples of Kindness:** You role-modeled empathy, compassion, and service, inspiring others to do the same.
- **Traditions Preserved:** The stories, rituals, and special events you nurtured deepened roots and kept memories alive.

ESFJ, embrace the extraordinary person you are, flaws and all. Continue learning, growing, and using your unique gifts to make a positive mark on the world. And always remember, the journey of being an ESFJ is one filled with heart, purpose, and the endless potential to make a difference.